Contributors

April Tompkins
Ashu Egbe
Katherine Scherer
Ernie Gammage
KM Bailey
Mike Cahoon
Phil Roberts
Neil Sheildman
Deborah Waffle
Jonathan Bockian
Stephen Weinstock
Fil A. Chavez
Rebecca Almeida
Adan Rhoades
J.G. Follansbee
Amelia Sterling
Stefan Vucak
T Geezer
Anita Lewis
Charylle Wolfe
Alexander Ellis

Photo Credits from Pexels:
Karola G
Clem Onojeghuo

COPYRIGHT © 2026
Review Tales Magazine - A Book Magazine for Indie Authors
This magazine may not be reproduced, either in part or in its entirety, in any form, by any means, without written permission from the publisher, with the exception of brief excerpts for purposes of radio, television, or published reviews. Although all possible means have been taken to ensure the accuracy of the material presented, Review Tales is not liable for any misinterpretation, misapplication or typographical errors. All rights, including the right of translation, are reserved.
Founder & Editor in Chief: S. Jeyran Main
Publisher: Review Tales Publishing & Editing Services
Print & Distribution: Ingram Spark
Designs: Pexels
ISBN 978-1-0699188-1-9 (Paperback)
ISBN 978-1-0699188-0-2 (Digital)
www.jeyranmain.com
For all inquiries, please contact us directly.

Editor's Note

Dear Readers,

Happy New Year, and welcome to the 17th edition of Book Article Magazine! As we step into a new year, it feels fitting to reflect on the power of stories—the ones we write, the ones we read, and the ones that shape us along the way. In this issue, our pages are filled with the voices of talented authors, each sharing their experiences, insights, and journeys in the world of writing and publishing.

From reflections on personal resilience in memoirs to the craft of writing novels, from navigating toxic relationships to blending love and business, this issue is a testament to the diversity of storytelling. You'll read about authors exploring history, memoir, fiction, and children's literature, and discover the unique perspectives that come from lives well-lived and stories well-told.

We celebrate the creativity, the courage, and the dedication of writers who open their hearts to their craft, who embrace both the triumphs and the challenges of the literary journey. Whether you're a writer seeking inspiration or a reader hungry for new voices, there is something here for you.

As we launch into this New Year, may these stories remind you of the power of words to entertain, educate, and connect us all. Here's to fresh pages, new ideas, and the enduring magic of storytelling in 2026.

Thank you for joining us, and happy reading!

Jeyran Main

Jeyran Main
Editor-in-Chief
Review Tales Magazine

Contents

Editor's Note — 01

Author Confessions — 03

Author Interview — 12

Words of Wisdom — 15

Editor's Pick — 23

Author Confessions

WRITE A SYMPHONY WITH WORDS

APRIL TOMPKINS

As a fiction writer who also writes songs, I strangely never considered the connection between the two. The differences? Definitely. If a songwriter's forte is lyrics, she needs to be able to convey emotion inside a tight little frame. Generally, song lyrics will contain only 8 to 10 words per line, at most. A songwriter needs to get to the point! While a fiction writer also needs to trim needless fluff, in my genre, exploring emotions is essential, so the narrative requires greater depth.

So, that's the big difference. What are the similarities?

I got to thinking about this a couple of weeks ago when one of my favorite instrumentals, "Love is Blue," popped up in my Spotify queue.

A well-done instrumental contains variations, such as pianissimos and crescendos. The composer is exploring emotions as a novelist would. The main character in a novel may have tender love scenes, and she may also have knockdown drag-out fights (or at least knockdown drag-out arguments).

But how does the writer arrange those movements? It matters. A story needs room to breathe. While a reader loves the dramatic scenes, for a novel to leave a lasting impression, it's essential to include reflective, quiet moments as well. A nd the quiet scenes give those dramatic bursts more impact. We see the main character's emotional buildup; we can feel it coming. "Ooh, I can't wait!" the reader thinks. "This is going to be exciting!"

Just as a musical composition can't consist of one note, neither can a work of fiction. When I first tried my hand at writing, I used the "this happened, then this happened" approach. No wonder I was a failure! Reading it back was like sitting in a lecture hall while a monotone-voiced speaker explained the history of the atom.

Variations—such as rhythm, melody, and even harmony—breathe life into a story. Don't be afraid to create a symphony.

Author Confessions

SHINING THE LIGHT: A LOVE LETTER TO RESILIENCE, IDENTITY, AND PURPOSE

ASHU EGBE

From the lush greenery of a Cameroonian village to the concrete pavements of European cities, Shining the Light is not merely a memoir—it is a tapestry of identity, endurance, and transformation. It is also my personal testimony, a story shaped by the trials of living with sickle cell disease (SCD) and the unyielding will to thrive beyond it.

As a child born with a lifelong illness, I learned early on that life would test me often and deeply. But I also learned, from my grandma Matop, that we can carry within us a light capable of piercing even the darkest tunnels. That belief is what gave birth to this book. It is my way of shining that light—not only on my own life but also on the countless lives that intersect with themes of struggle, self-discovery, and the search for meaning.

One reviewer aptly called this book "a lantern for all of us navigating pain, identity, and purpose." That metaphor resonates with me. My story—woven with love, cultural memory, academic pursuits, and creative reinvention—is not unique because of its pain but because of its insistence on hope.

Shining the Light is deeply personal, but its messages are universal. Whether it is the bond between a grandmother and grandson or the experience of leaving home to seek something greater, readers from all backgrounds will find a reflection of themselves in these pages.

My journey from rural Bachuo-Ntai to the University of Birmingham and beyond has been shaped not just by intellect but by purpose. A trained engineer and passionate storyteller, I have walked the tightrope between logic and creativity.

One reviewer described the book as "a love letter to the resilience of the human spirit." Another noted its impact as "a light for all of us on finding our purpose and being part of something bigger than ourselves."

As a sickle cell advocate and genetic counsellor, I believe in telling stories that go beyond statistics to touch hearts. As a filmmaker, I've learned that narrative has the power to change minds.

To quote another thoughtful reviewer, this book is for "anyone who appreciates epics of triumph against the odds... and finds inspiration in individuals who use their experiences to empower others."

In the words of my late grandmother Matop—"No matter how far you travel, never forget the way home."

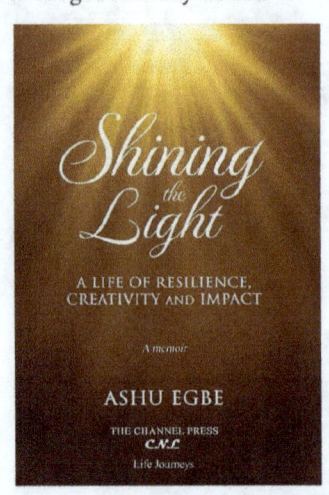

Author Confessions

PRACTICING GRATITUDE A LIFESTYLE CHANGE FOR HEALTH AND HAPPINESS

KATHERINE SCHERER

Have you ever caught yourself vigorously complaining about something you felt you couldn't do anything about? Have you ever told yourself you needed to quit whining, only to find yourself in the same old complaining scenario the very next day? I'm not talking about dissatisfaction that motivates us to come up with creative ideas or solutions. And I don't mean ordinary challenges that help us grow. I'm talking about needless complaining that serves absolutely no purpose because you can't do anything about it. Or maybe it isn't you who's the habitual complainer—perhaps it's someone you know.

Whether it's your own negativity or someone else's, negativity can turn a sunny day into a gloomy one. Needless complaining day after day can stifle the greatness of the human spirit and lead to feelings of hopelessness and despair. Negativity that goes unchecked can lead to a self-destructive lifestyle that robs you and those around you of positive emotions, optimism, and a feeling of connection to all life.

It would be great if everyone were full of energy and moving through life without resistance. In reality, many of us feel exhausted, need to lower our stress levels, and could really use more joy in our daily lives. The good news is that we can achieve all of this just by creating a happier frame of mind. Adopting an attitude of gratitude can create a happier outlook on life. By choosing to live in gratitude, we bless what is working in our lives rather than lament what is not. Recent research shows that the practice of gratitude can reduce stress, increase life satisfaction, and boost vitality.

By practicing gratitude, we make a conscious effort to look for the good in our lives. Practicing gratitude is a lifestyle choice that we must make if we want to feel healthier and happier. Replacing old habits with new ones is sometimes hard work, but the gratitude habit will take root over time if we cultivate it.

Here are a few simple suggestions to make it easy for you to practice your new habit of gratitude until it becomes a lifestyle change:

1. As soon as you open your eyes in the morning, remind yourself how blessed you are and say "thank you."
2. Slow down until you begin to notice the blessings all around you—the miracle in a smile, a beautiful sunset, and the first spring flower.
3. Every night, ask yourself what this day has brought to you.
4. Every night, ask yourself what you have given in return.

Remember the words of Helen Keller: "Keep your face to the sunshine and You cannot see the shadows."

Author Confessions

WRITING SONGS AND FICTION

ERNIE GAMMAGE

I've been a songwriter since I was fifteen years old. Now, at eighty, I write fiction. What's the difference? What are the commonalities? Is one format easier than another? Which format do I prefer?

Writing a song, even though it may (and usually does) have an emotional component, is like baking a cake: you follow a recipe. There are rhyme patterns to attend to, verse/chorus/bridge patterns to follow, and, if you're looking to get airplay or broadcast/streaming opportunities, time limits. Songs have structures that define everything about them, including content. In other words, songs have constraints—big time!

Fiction, on the other hand, has none of these issues. I'm not counting three- or six-act story structures as constraints because those serve only as the web in which a story is caught. In fiction, the rabbit holes of plot can lead anywhere, for any length. This is not to say that wrangling with this freedom is not tricky. It is, and it's what editing is about. Still, the notion that there are few external constraints in writing fiction is liberating, allowing an author to explore the wildest limits of their imagination.

The common thread running through songs and fiction is stories. Some songwriters specialize in "story songs"—think The Wreck of the Edmund Fitzgerald by Gordon Lightfoot. I used to think I didn't write story songs, but listen to Carmen Wear Your Red Dress Tonight on my YouTube channel. If that's not a story song, I don't know what is.

Fiction is, of course, a story—a lengthy story. It's stories—told in front of a cave around a campfire, heard from a stage, or read in your favorite book—that connect us, inform us about ourselves, and bind us. Let's keep writing them in every format!

If you'd like to hear some of the songs I've written over the past 65 years, check out my YouTube channel, where you'll find 80+ songs in multiple genres: https://www.youtube.com/@erniegammagevideo/videos.

Author Confessions

ENDURING THROUGH WORDS: A WRITER'S JOURNEY FROM LIFE TO PRINT

KM BAILEY

Sometimes life gets in the way, but that's a good thing.

I was always fascinated by history: different experiences, different perspectives, different societies. If I could leap into a book and unlock its secrets, I was never happier. My grandfather Tom inspired and fed this passion, sharing his love of books, music, and poetry with all his grandchildren, always looking for the uplifting and the life-affirming, and raging at the world (literally shouting at his television) when he thought people could and should do better. He introduced me to Shakespeare and Dickens, Keats and Orwell, and, whilst studying at London University, I added my own choices to this canon: Mary Shelley, Graham Greene, and Joseph Conrad being particular favourites.

I don't remember not writing. Anything and everything that popped into my head, I wrote down. It went hand in hand with the business of living, and through it all, I kept on scribbling. But the simple truth is that sometimes life gets in the way. That's why it has taken me a brief twenty years to get to print. The process was rhythmic: research, write, review, rewrite, then repeat and repeat. You would probably call me a perfectionist, but my thinking was simple: if I was going to do this, I wanted to do it well. I also loved the research; delving deep into places and times that are not my own was fascinating and all-consuming. And the business of living? That was ultimately a really good thing—my life as a student, actor, editor, mother, wife, cultural officer, and primary school teacher has made me dig deeper, think harder, and write better.

My novel Requiem is set in a quiet English village on the eve of WW1 and follows the lives of the working-class Baxter siblings as they navigate the war years and its immediate aftermath. This is not a novel about the horrors of trench warfare but rather a reflection on the unseen wounds of conflict—the quiet devastations that affected so many in this, the first truly global conflict. It is a novel about shifting times, of class and gender, of innocence lost, and the burden of survival. But it is also a book about hope and, ultimately, the indomitable strength of the human spirit to endure.

Author Confessions

FLIPPING THE SWITCH
MAKING THE JUMP FROM
WRITER TO AUTHOR

MIKE CAHOON

As I barrel toward the launch of my debut novel, I find myself reflecting on the long and winding road that brought me here. A lot of days and nights were spent clacking away at a keyboard, staring at a blank screen, and willing the words to come out. Writing can be a challenge, just like any creative endeavor. But in the end, you have this creation that you can point to and be proud of, and that helps justify it all.

What's harder to come to terms with is that writing is only half the battle. What no one tells you about becoming an author is how difficult everything else is—learning to balance your time, being a self-promoter, a marketer, an editor, a social media manager, a website designer, and more. The ever-growing list of skills you're forced to learn inevitably begins to weigh you down.

One thing I found that helped me the most during all that grinding away was mentally flipping the switch—learning to call myself an author, to think of my writing and all that work as part of the job. It's tempting to get lost in the romance of being a writer. But writing is work, and if you think of it as just a hobby or a side project, all the nitty-gritty bits of publishing can feel like chewing a mouthful of nails.

It's easy to become disillusioned or distracted by other endeavors, stories, or interests. But if you can tell yourself, I am an author, truly believe this is all part of it, and recognize that it's all important, you can find a real purpose behind the minutia. The often-grueling process can become a challenge, a skill—one that is more passion than burden. I know it helped me, and I hope this makes sense to some of those who are struggling to make the leap from writer to author.

Author Confessions

FINDING THE VOICE OF THE 1920S.

PHIL ROBERTS

My novel, The Luckiest Fool on Earth: The Twisted Yarn of America's Greatest Flagpole Sitter, Alvin "Shipwreck" Kelly, occurs primarily in the Roaring 1920s and the Depression 1930s. Making sure the voice and idioms fit the era was a particularly complex problem. I felt that the vernacular had to be balanced with everyday talk. I consciously chose to use slang sparingly, but I also wanted the ballyhoo of the medicine-show talker and the circus-barker lingo to shine through in the narrative.

The backstories of the trio of main characters informed my choices. The hero, the "cool center" of my story, comes across as an "everyman" with a faint nautical bent in his simple, likable vocabulary. The secondary, prominent personality in the tale is a whip-smart, college-educated newspaperman who favored big words. The third member of the triad, Alvin's wife, had a trauma-filled past that contributed to her patois of flapper/grifter slang.

Let me give you a few examples of the language of the day that I repurposed. Most of these were cobbled together from hipster jazz, period movies, and the soundscapes of the golden age of radio drama.

The phrase "She knows her onions" means "She's wise." It comes from a popular 1926 song by The Happiness Boys (plus at least four other jazz outfits) before being put on acetate by cornetist and bandleader Red Nichols. I use it when Alvin is explaining what his wife is feeling as they travel across America.

"That comes straight from the feedbag" is a throwaway line during a party sequence in a Thin Man movie starring William Powell and Myrna Loy. The statement infers that what follows is raw, unpolished, and unfiltered. I use it when Kelly's manager riffs the line while briefing a crowd of newspaper reporters. I pair it with "This ain't no phonus-balonus."

It's little details like these that really bring the people to life. I can hear them talking in my brain, and that's the effect I was going for.

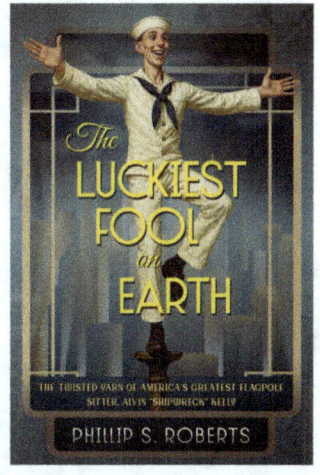

Author Confessions

KILLING YOUR DARLINGS (AND LOVING IT!) A LESSON IN EDITING

NEIL SHEILDMAN

"Young man, care to explain this?"

I was a young man, maybe twelve or thirteen, and for an English project, my teacher had assigned us to write a horror story for Halloween. While most kids wrote about ghosts, haunted houses, and death, I decided, "Hey, if I'm going to write a story, I'm gonna write a killer horror story."

Here's the story.

A girl kidnapped her crush and buried him alive in her walls. Then each night, when he's scratching at the wall, trying to escape, she fell asleep knowing that he was close to her.

It was a brilliant idea!

At least I thought so.

My English teacher? Not so much.

My English teacher met with me and said, "You need to rewrite this."

"How?" I asked.

"Kill your darlings," my English teacher responded.

"What darlings?" I asked.

"Make it better. Edit it. Make sure it's not…this…" She set the paper on the table with a hard thud.

Kill your darlings. I learned that when it comes time to edit, I had to ask myself, "What if this person died right now? How would that affect my story?" I learned that when you write the dreaded first draft, what you write is not what people are going to read. In that first draft, what's on the paper is there for you to edit. And it is our job to go in there and shape the story into its final form for our readers.

And the best part? It's fun!

You will read passages that will make you think, Wow! I wrote that?!

However, you will read passages where you will think, Whoa…I wrote that? Do I even know how to write?!

The secret is to keep moving forward and have fun! And remember, no one will read your work until you say they can. So, kill your darlings! Don't be afraid to go in and take them out! Kill a character that was deemed "essential" when you started, and see where the story goes! What happens if you take out one of the main characters? What happens if the sidekick is thrust into the spotlight? Where does your story go from here? That is for you, the author, to decide.

And for those of you wondering, I killed the buried-alive boy in the second draft. The girl who did it kept his corpse under her bed, where she would cuddle with it each night. You should've seen my English teacher's face when she read the new story. She never told me to kill my darlings again.

Author Confessions

HOW MEMOIRS SAVED ME
DEBORAH WAFFLE

When my daughter's illness worsened, no matter how many doctors or medical facilities we visited, I started reading memoirs. My favorite memoirs told stories about people who, after experiencing some sort of traumatic struggle, chose not to give up on life but to take their lives in new and positive directions. I'd share these stories with my daughter, Kelsey, and tell her, "Someday you'll find your something good!"

I was devastated when my daughter passed away suddenly at the age of 29. It wasn't fair that she died before having an opportunity to find her "something good." I struggled to get through each day with consuming grief. The person I saw in the mirror looked like a stranger. Who was she without her daughter?

But I kept thinking about the real-life stories I'd read over the last 10 years. I wondered if I was strong enough to emulate all those people. So, I continued reading memoirs and clung to them like a life preserver.

At the same time, I started writing letters to Kelsey because I missed her so much. I also wrote an informative article about her illness and planned on trying to get it published in a magazine. Gradually, these two very different forms of writing began to merge. I started to see a theme and the same narrative arc necessary for a memoir to take shape. For the next year, I sat at my kitchen table and wrote as if my life depended on it. This is how My Grief Jar: Still Growing After the Loss of My Daughter came to be.

When I read my first inspirational memoir, I never could have imagined the impact it would have on my future. This genre gave me a foundation to build on as I learned how to live in a world without my daughter. The lessons in these books were like a road map showing me a path toward a new beginning.

Author Interview

What Was Forbidden: a Venice Ghetto mystery by Jonathan Bockian

When did you first realize you wanted to be a writer?

It was probably sometime in college when I first developed novel envy. At that time, I had what a friend called "delusions of adequacy" about many youthful aspirations. It wasn't until I was in my late 40s or early 50s, while I was in the thick of practicing law, that my desire to write went from a vague fantasy to an intentio,n and I began taking evening writing classes.

How do you schedule your life when you're writing?

When I wrote What Was Forbidden, I tried to write for at least two hours each morning, often seven days a week. By the afternoon, whatever creativity I had would congeal into a substance that wouldn't flow. I was disciplined, perhaps compulsive, about finding time to write every day, and fortunate to be able to devote that much time to writing. It amazes me that anyone can write creatively in the evening after putting in their hours on a day job.

What would you say is your interesting writing quirk?

It's hard for me to imagine that anything about how I write is unusual or interesting. On someone's advice, I eventually took to reading aloud everything I write, and sometimes I use the "read aloud" review function in Word to listen to my writing in another voice, to try to hear it a little more objectively.

How did you get your book published?

What Was Forbidden got published when I accepted that it wasn't going to be published by an established press. I was able to find an agent only after a long search, as happens to most writers. My agent (now my former agent) worked hard to interest an established publisher in the book. Unfortunately, even the many acquisition editors who said nice things about the book declined to buy it. But from all the comments along the way, which suggested how the book fell short, I found ways to revise and improve my writing, so the process was valuable to me.

What do you like to do when you're not writing?

Visit our children and grandchildren, read, participate in community affairs, doom scroll, walk, cook, and try to interest people in reading my book.

THE QARAQ AND THE MAYA FACTOR
BY STEPHEN WEINSTOCK

Author Interview

As a child, what did you want to do when you grew up?

My interests have always been in the performing arts, from childhood through young adulthood and beyond. I acted in plays in high school, learned all the theater jobs in college, went to grad school in stage directing, morphed into a theater composer, wrote experimental works, musicals, and operas, and taught at NYU's Musical Theater Writing Program. Later, I settled into a career as a dance accompanist, improvising for modern dance at the Fame School in NYC. When I hit the top of my game, creating dance music, I realized I wanted to write fantasy novels. Talk about drama!

When did you first realize you wanted to be a writer?

I always wrote stories and filled dozens of journals. One year I had the idea for a novel with small chapters that read like deja vus, then accrue into a past life narrative. I was a composer, so I put the idea aside. Then I had a revelation to structure the book after the 1001 Nights, each past life fragment like the part of a story Scheherazade leaves unfinished. My ideas broadened the work into much more than fragments, but the long accumulation of a past life history remained. I had to write this work; I became a writer.

Where did you get your information or idea for your book?

I did much research into reincarnation, since it's the central concept of the series, The Reincarnation Chronicles. I even experienced past life regressions! But the greatest inspiration came from research into The Thousand and One Nights. There is no book like it; there is no single edition that is the original or correct version of the anthology. The history of Arabic literature is fascinating; it helped me appreciate the culture. I'm so in love with the Nights that I gave my characters dozens of past lives, creating an edition of the Nights, and discovering it has magical properties.

Author Interview

Unused Towels by Fil A. Chavez

What inspired the title Unused Towels?

Unused towels are a metaphor for unused talents. When I visited home, my mother did not allow me to use the good towels; "they were for company." When she died, we found over 10 unused towels neatly stacked where no one had ever used them. When I die, I do not want anyone to find that I left any talents that God loaned me unused.

Can you share a moment or chapter in the book that was particularly challenging to write, and why?

The parts dealing with suicide, not only because of my experiences but also because of the daily news regarding how many veterans, people older than 75, teenagers, and celebrities have taken their lives. The number of those committing suicide continues to grow; a recent 60 Minutes story revealed that farmers are 3.5 times more likely to commit suicide than the general population.

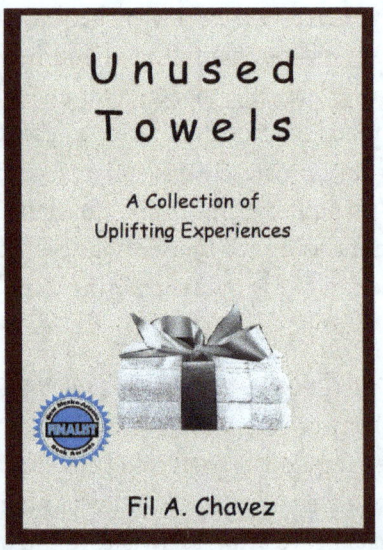

How did your experiences as a veteran shape the stories and perspectives in Unused Towels?

Empathy for my brothers and sisters who sacrificed and served in combat. I was sent to Yale for a year to learn Mandarin Chinese and therefore never experienced the direct horrors of war like these heroes and heroines; this makes me care even more.

What advice would you give friends or family members trying to support someone experiencing suicidal thoughts?

First, be 100% honest! If you genuinely care enough to take real action to show it, do it! If not, please do not start and then give up for any reason; not following through with your actions will likely accelerate their distress! Second, initiate a conversation about something important to them, then let them take the lead. Do not offer your solutions to their problems!

Do you have future projects planned that will continue exploring themes of mental health, personal growth, or humor in difficult situations?

My focus is now on getting the word out about suicidal depression.

If you could give one key takeaway to every reader picking up Unused Towels, what would it be?

God's love is unconditional! Get busy fully using your God-given skills, for yourself and for others!

Words of Wisdom

A STRANGER'S NUDGE
Rebecca Almeida

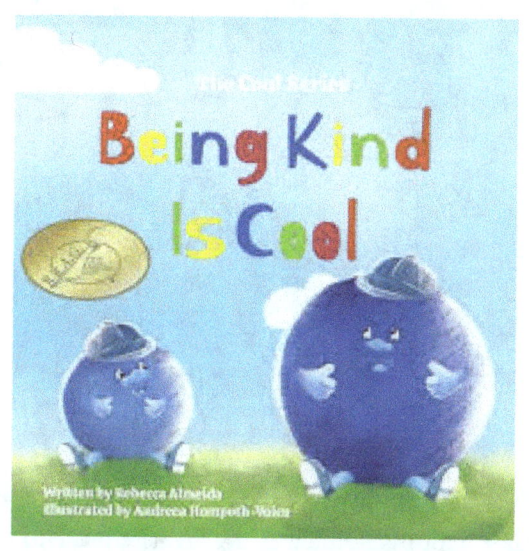

My author journey started a year ago, but really over a decade ago. Let me explain. I was attending New Jersey City University (NJCU) for my Master's Degree in Early Childhood Education. My whole life, I wanted to be a psychologist, but life led me to teaching instead. Looking back, I'm glad for this change of heart because it has led me to become an author today. During one of my graduate courses, we had an interesting assignment: write a children's book. We had to pick our intended audience and choose two subjects we would focus on. I picked toddlers, math, and social studies. I sat down that night and wrote, "Being Kind is Cool." I wrote my now multi-award-winning Children's Picture Book a decade ago for a homework assignment.

I don't remember writing it, but I do remember my thoughts after finishing it… "This is really good." The next thing I remember is the teacher asking who wants to come up and read their book. I was the first person to raise my hand. I don't remember reading it, but I do remember what one classmate said. "That was really good. You should publish it." That was reassuring because I knew I thought it was good, but maybe I was being biased. Now I knew someone else thought it was good, and that made all the difference. I went home that night and thought I was too busy with schooling to publish a book. I put the book away in a folder and said I would revisit it.

Years later, I remembered I had a book in a folder I wanted to publish. I looked and looked. The folder was gone. I gave up. Time passed. Years later, I decided to sit down and try to rewrite the words I had written years before. If you were to ask me today how accurate my recollection of the original work is to my published work now, I couldn't tell you. It is definitely similar, but I wonder if the original work was better.

My current life could be very different right now. If a stranger hadn't nudged me. Suppose I didn't take her or my book seriously. If I didn't believe the book was worth rewriting. To this day, I am grateful for that stranger and also for the belief in myself that I had something worth sharing.

If that stranger happens to be reading this right now… thank you.

REBIRTH GAVE BIRTH TO WRITING

Adan Rhoades

As a child, the top of the mountain where my grandfather built his home was my favorite place to vacation. I'd awaken at the break of dawn and stand outside to witness and be immersed in the visual splendor. The morning fog hovered below it and two neighboring mountaintops, creating a sense of standing atop the world. The sea of cloud-white covered the entirety of the remaining world. As the light of the sun breached the morning sky, warming the fog below, I would soon be engulfed in dense cloud as it rose above it all. When all of the fog had risen and dissipated, the world around me was revealed. I can think of no better analogy to an endeavor that led to the transformation of my perceptions of writing from that of a utility to that of passion.

Like a dense fog, the effects of early childhood abuse had overshadowed my ability to live a life with untroubled pursuits. Life had a way of slipping by—a life darkened by hyper-vigilance and relentless internal turmoil. Entering my senior years, I found a certain relief which enabled me to journal my experiences, and a sense of newfound peace and healing emerged as the fog lifted. Soon after, journaling was no longer enough.

The thing is, I had no idea that lurking below the fog was a world with passions that included writing. There were hints, such as moments, for reasons I don't fully understand, when, in an almost trance-like state, I would communicate through utterance or written word a profound message. I would hear from others that I had a gift, but I had/have difficulty believing. However, the journal turned into a memoir, and that memoir evolved with a newfound passion. And so, my first formal indie book, The Crumbling Shield of Defiance, is both a chronicle of the transformations of my life and a passion to write.

I don't know why this capacity, this interest, this passion, remained hidden from me for so many decades, only to emerge now. Perhaps in my quest to free my soul from the stifling grips of trauma through a willingness to bare that soul for the world to see, a spark inside simply wished to be represented in good light. Or perhaps it has always been there and was merely masked by self-doubt and fear. Nonetheless, here it is, and it is growing.

Take it from me: a capacity toward expression is a gift to the soul. Now, I need to make time to listen to my heart and allow it to express itself, and to write again.

Words of Wisdom

HOW AI HELPS ME BOOST MY PRODUCTIVITY AND CREATIVITY

J.G. Follansbee

Generative AI has transformed the way I work. Almost from the day ChatGPT was launched in late 2022, I experimented with how it could improve my productivity and spark creativity. As a working person, I can only devote so much time to writing daily, and AI has helped me make the most of that time and energy.

According to Bookbub, less than half of writers admit to using AI, though I believe the number is larger. I want to encourage acceptance of AI as a creative augmenter by sharing how I've used it.

Writing – After discovering ChatGPT, a friend suggested Claude AI, tuned for writing. Generating ideas without tired cliches has relieved some of the pain of writing. I've uploaded raw notes and asked AI to organize them, suggest story structures, or add new scenes. AI lets me reflect on ideas quickly and provides near-instant analysis of drafts, offering feedback without judgment.

Images – I have no talent in graphic arts, but AI tools like ChatGPT's image generator, Leonardo AI, and NightCafe let me visualize ideas. Text-to-image prompting is almost magical, helping me test world-building and character-building ideas graphically.

Programming – At my job, I use programming to automate repetitive tasks. My experience with Perl and MySQL helped me with Power Automate scripts and VBA applications. MS Copilot has saved me at least 50 percent of coding time, and incorporating GPT into simple scripts helps summarize long emails and complex PDFs.

While writers have a right to worry about copyright use in AI training, generative AI is too useful to ignore. Experimenting with free accounts on ChatGPT or using Copilot can improve your productivity and creativity.

J.G. Follansbee writes climate science fiction, fantasy fiction, and maritime history in Seattle. He recently published The Stowaway's Secret, a YA historical fiction work, and blogs at jgfollansbee.com.

Words of Wisdom

BREAKING FREE: RECLAIMING YOUR VOICE AFTER NARCISSISTIC ABUSE

Amelia Sterling

For many, the journey of writing begins not with ambition but with survival. My book, Break Free from Narcissistic Abuse: Your Guide to Recover from Toxic Relationships, Reclaim Your Confidence & Embrace a Life Filled with Peace & Joy, was born from such a place. Writing it was not only an act of creation but an act of healing—a way to transform personal pain into a message of hope for others walking a similar path.

Narcissistic relationships are often shrouded in silence. Victims can feel unseen, unheard, and deeply diminished, unsure of why they are losing their sense of self. Like countless others, I reached a breaking point, sitting across from a friend who reminded me that I deserved to be valued. That simple but profound truth sparked a journey of discovery and restoration that ultimately inspired me to share my story through writing.

In the book, I explore the subtle yet damaging traits of narcissism—control, manipulation, lack of empathy—and their devastating impact on self-esteem and mental health. But this is not a narrative of despair. Instead, it is a roadmap to healing, filled with practical strategies such as setting healthy boundaries, rebuilding self-worth, and practicing self-care.

Writing this book also reshaped my identity as an author. It taught me that storytelling is not just about words on a page; it's about giving voice to experiences that others may be too afraid to name. For me, writing became a form of advocacy, ensuring that no one else would feel as isolated as I once did.

For anyone navigating a toxic relationship or seeking to reclaim their life, my message is simple: your story matters. Healing is possible. And sometimes, the act of reading or writing is the first step toward rediscovering yourself.

Words of Wisdom

BEWARE THE PROCRASTINATION DEMONS

Stefan Vucak

You are sitting at your writing desk, chewing the end of that pen, staring at the notebook or PC, wondering what the hell to do next. The words don't want to come, your mind is blank, and every distraction suddenly seems appealing—sunshine outside, yard work, washing the car, or a video you've been meaning to watch. Anything but facing that stubborn piece of writing. And if you give in, a procrastination demon has already won.

Writing is hard work—lonely, stiffening, and frustrating when you hit that mental pothole. We've all been there. Sometimes a pause helps, but often it becomes an easy escape. Accept that there are moments when words simply won't flow. If they won't come, they won't come. The real questions are: How do you get moving again? And how did you fall into the hole in the first place? Understanding both gives you the first rung out.

The truth behind falling in is simple: you probably don't have a detailed outline, or you're relying on a vague mental picture and hoping it develops as you go. There's no mystery. Short stories may not require outlines, but even a few dot points help. For longer work, a solid outline prevents the spiral into procrastination. You wouldn't build a house without a plan—don't write a book without one.

Still, outline or not, everyone eventually hits a snag that freezes their writing. That's part of the job. But procrastinating won't write the page for you. To restart, revisit your outline. Look at the plot thread that has unraveled or the dead end you never tied up—often the hidden cause of your block. Work out how to weave it back into shape. Sometimes it's simple; sometimes it requires reworking part of the story.

And sometimes, the solution is simply allowing your mind to freewheel. Don't panic about the demons. Sit back, breathe, and trust that eventually, the words will return.

Words of Wisdom

BEWARE THE PROCRASTINATION DEMONS
T Geezer

I'm an old man, past seventy-five, and only recently began writing novels. Since turning seventy, I've written half a dozen books. I went to college more years ago than most of you have lived.

Though I readily admit to not being a great literary author—I never took a creative writing course, not during college or since—I did take some very sage advice from a former boss: shut up unless you know what you are talking about. In the case of creative writing, the advice turns into something simple: write about what you know.

Before you go through all the preparations—creating a storyline, outlining the progressions, developing characters, and so much more—figure out what you know and what you don't. I spent most of my adult life as a traveling salesman, working for an air conditioning and heating manufacturer. Yes, I know a lot about air conditioning, but more importantly, I know a lot about human relationships. Hence, I write about human relationships, the small interactions and odd conversations that make stories feel alive.

If you know about automobiles, create a tale that includes some of the things about cars that bring your story to life. The creative part is figuring out the story itself. Sometimes the key is simply to begin with an idea of where you want the story to go, even if you don't yet understand the entire tale. Just because what you've written doesn't seem to take you anywhere, don't toss it. A dead end in one project doesn't mean it won't be useful in the next.

And don't fret about "writer's block"; it doesn't exist. What does exist is stress, and stressing about what to write next will block you from being open and honest with yourself. Once you allow your creative mind to do its job, the block disappears, and words suddenly appear on the page. They might not lead where you first intended, but they're your words, from your mind, and therefore part of your story. Tell it.

Words of Wisdom

HOW I ACCIDENTALLY BECAME AN AUTHOR

Anita Lewis

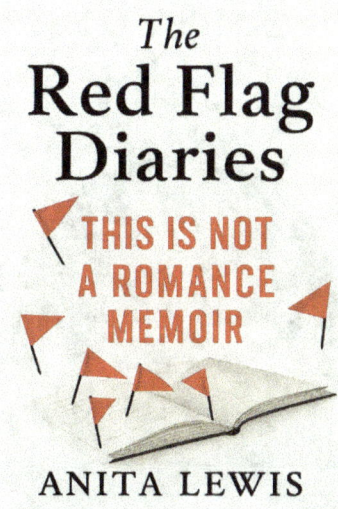

I never expected to become an author. Writing a book wasn't on my list of goals, but one day I found myself flipping through old journals and realized there was too much material to keep tucked away. The stories, reflections, and even the sarcastic notes to myself felt alive on the page. Maybe these weren't just private memories; they were the foundation of something bigger.

That spark became The Red Flag Diaries: This Is Not a Romance Memoir. My book doesn't follow the typical path of a love story. In fact, it's the opposite. It's about two toxic relationships I stayed in for all the wrong reasons: obligation, guilt, fear, and the belief that walking away wasn't possible.

The challenge was telling those stories without making them unbearably heavy. My answer was humor—specifically sarcasm. Humor carried me through those years, and it allowed me to share my experiences on the page without turning them bleak. Readers deserve honesty, but they also deserve a reason to keep turning the pages.

Writing a memoir also meant facing my own flaws. It wasn't just about what others had done to me, but what I had allowed by ignoring the glaring red flags. That self-reflection was uncomfortable, but it made the story real. People don't connect to a polished version of life; they connect to the messy, complicated truths.

Finishing the book was only half the journey. Publishing brought its own learning curve: formatting, cover design, ads, and marketing. It was overwhelming at times, but holding the finished book in my hands made the long nights and endless edits worth it.

I may not have planned on becoming an author, but I'm grateful I listened to the voice that told me my story was worth sharing. Sometimes the best stories are the ones we never expect to write.

WRITING THE BUSINESS OF US: TURNING A BOOK INTO A LIFELINE FOR ENTREPRENEURIAL COUPLES

Charylle Wolfe

When I began writing The Couplepreneur Code, I didn't set out to create just another business book. I wanted to write a survival guide for couples who dared to mix love with entrepreneurship—a combination that can be as thrilling as it is treacherous.

My journey as an author has always been tied to collaboration. I co-authored several business bestsellers early in my career, learning the mechanics of publishing, promotion, and deadlines. But behind those professional wins, I kept noticing a quiet, persistent problem: couples in business together were burning out—not just financially, but emotionally. Traditional business books offered strategies for scaling, marketing, and leadership, but none addressed the "business of us," the fragile yet powerful intersection where marriage and enterprise meet.

That realization came from lived experience. For 32 years my husband and I have been married, and for much of that journey we've also been business partners—navigating everything from traditional companies to less conventional ventures, often at the same time. We've weathered seasons of abundance and seasons of stress, moments when the spreadsheets made sense but our relationship did not. The truth is, being in business with your spouse isn't just a professional decision—it's a lifestyle. Writing this book meant putting words to the lessons we've learned the hard way and creating a framework that could spare other couples unnecessary heartbreak.

Books change lives because they allow readers to see themselves in the pages. For me, the act of writing has been just as transformative. It reminded me that the best businesses aren't built on spreadsheets or marketing hacks—they're built on strong partnerships. If my work sparks even one couple to fight for both their love and their livelihood, then the late nights at my keyboard were worth it.

Editor's Pick

THE RADICAL REALISM OF JESUS BY JEYRAN MAIN

In an age of skepticism and distraction, The Radical Realism of Jesus invites readers to rediscover Christ—not as distant theology but as a model of grounded realism, ethics, and relational wisdom. Instead of abstract doctrine, this book presents Jesus as the ultimate realist: historically rooted, philosophically sound, and relationally transformative. Through His actions and parables, He shows what it means to live truthfully—to love with discernment, act with justice, and recognize the sacred in daily life.

Engaging modern philosophical traditions, this work bridges ancient insight with contemporary thought. Whether you come as a believer, seeker, or student of philosophy, it offers an intellectually honest and ethically grounded framework for understanding faith. It challenges the idea that faith and reason are opposed, revealing how Christ's realism transcends both doubt and dogma.

Thoughtful and timely, this book calls readers to see Jesus not only as a historical figure but as a living paradigm for truth, ethics, and hope today.

TILL I BLEED NO MORE BY ALEXANDER ELLIS

Discovered in a dusty attic and believed to be the last surviving piece of a mysterious 1920s "Starter Kit," The Half-Full-Glass User's Manual is a playful, profound, and occasionally preposterous guide to living with more joy, balance, and awareness—one sip at a time.

At its center is The Glass—a curious device (or metaphor?) reminding us to take more mindful, optimistic swigs from whatever fills our cup—paired with The Consciousness, a state shaped through ritual, reflection, and humor.

Whether you're a seeker, skeptic, or simply someone who enjoys a good read with a twist of wonder, this manual offers a fresh way to view life. The Glass is now before you... drink from it or pass.